EVERYDAY SCIENCE

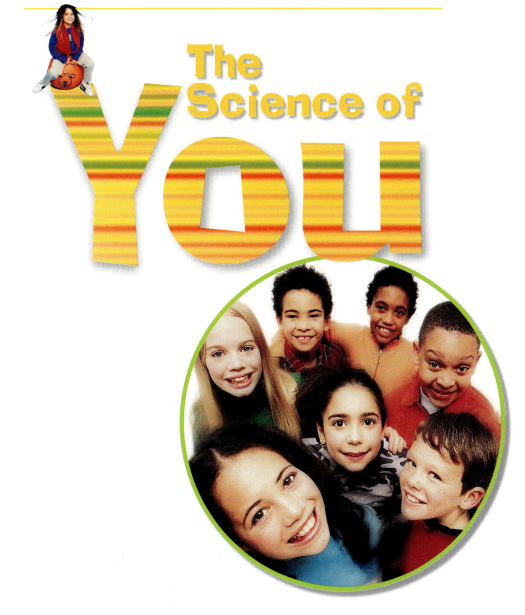

The Science of YOU

Kate Boehm Jerome

PICTURE CREDITS
Cover: (background) © Digital Stock (title inset and foreground image) © Digital Vision, Inc.
Page 1, 4 (top left), 5 (lower right), 6 (top left): © Digital Vision, Inc.; pages 2-3, top borders on pages 4-5, 6-7, 8-9, 10-11, 12-13, 14-15, 16-17, 18-19, 20-21, background on pages 22-23, 24: Herman Adler Design; pages 4-5: © Albano Guatti/CORBIS; page 5 (top right): © Jean Shapiro Cantu; page 6 (lower left): © Quest/Photo Researchers, Inc.; pages 6-7: © David Turnley/CORBIS; page 7 (mid right), 8-9, 10-11, 23: © gettyimages; page 8 (top left) © Bob Llewellyn/Pictor International/Picture Quest; page 9: © Stockbyte/PictureQuest; page 11: © Mark Clark/SPL/Photo Researchers, Inc.; page 12 (top left), page 14 (top left), page 16 (top left and lower left), page 18 (top left), page 20 (top left): © PhotoDisc, Inc.; page 12 (lower left): © Bob Daemmrich/The Image Works; page 13 (top left): © Michael Newman/PhotoEdit, Inc.; page 13 (full page), 19 (top right), 20 (lower left): © David Young-Wolff/PhotoEdit Inc.; pages 14-15: © Charles Gupton/Corbis; page 15 (top right): © Simon DesRochers/Masterfile; page 17: © Philippe Plailly/SPL/Photo Researchers, Inc.; pages 18-19: © Firefly Productions/CORBIS; page 21: © R. Nissen-Petzer/Pictor International Ltd./PictureQuest.

Produced through the worldwide resources of the National Geographic Society, John M. Fahey, Jr., President and Chief Executive Officer; Gilbert M. Grosvenor, Chairman of the Board; Nina D. Hoffman, Executive Vice President and President, Books and Education Publishing Group.

PREPARED BY NATIONAL GEOGRAPHIC SCHOOL PUBLISHING
Ericka Markman, Senior Vice President and President Children"s Books and Education Publishing Group; Steve Mico, Vice President, Editorial Director; Marianne Hiland, Executive Editor; Jim Hiscott, Design Manager; Ruth Goldberg, Photo Editor; Kristin Hanneman, Illustrations Manager; Matt Wascavage, Manager of Publishing Services; Sean Philpotts, Production Manager; Jane Ponton, Production Artist.

MANUFACTURING AND QUALITY MANAGEMENT
Christopher A. Liedel, Chief Financial Officer; Phillip L. Schlosser, Director; Clifton M. Brown III, Manager.

PROGRAM DEVELOPMENT
Kate Boehm Jerome

CONSULTANT/REVIEWER
Dr. James Symansky, E. Desmond Lee Professor of Science Education, University of Missouri-St. Louis; Glen Phelan, science writer, Palatine, Illinois; Patrick McGeehan, researcher, Washington, D.C.

BOOK DEVELOPMENT
Amy Sarver; Thomas Nieman, Inc.

BOOK DESIGN
Herman Adler Design

Published by the National Geographic Society
1145 17th Street, N.W.
Washington, D.C. 20036-4688

ISBN: 0-7922-8629-4

11 10 09
10 9 8 7 6 5

Contents

The Science of You

You already know that you are an amazing person. But it's not just your wonderful personality. Your body itself is a remarkable machine.

Lots of information has been written on the subject of "you." The big picture of how your body systems work together is important to understand. But sometimes the details interest us the most.

This is a book about some of the little things that you might wonder about your body. It answers the kinds of questions that pop into your head when you least expect it. Let's say, for example, you are on your way to get a haircut . . .

when you
suddenly
wonder . . .

Why don't haircuts hurt?

Snip, snip—the scissors fly around your head. Your hair grows from living cells. But the hair that's cut is not alive. What's the story here?

Each hair on your head grows from a root that is under your skin. The root produces hair cells in a special tube called a **follicle.** When new hair cells are made at the root, they push older hair cells up the follicle.

As older hair cells move toward the surface of your skin, they change. They squeeze together and harden. Then they die. The strand of hair that comes out of your head does not have living cells in it. That's why a haircut doesn't hurt!

Hair follicle (magnified)

You probably have about 100,000 hairs on your head right now. Hair strands constantly grow, fall out, and then start to grow again. It usually does this in different stages. That's why you don't lose all of your hair at once.

People like to change their hair colors and styles. Sometimes the results are very interesting. In fact, you might be wide-eyed and staring at one of these creations . . .

when you
suddenly
wonder . . .

Why do people blink?

Go ahead. Stare eye-to-eye with a friend. Try not to blink. You may win the contest, but it's only a matter of time before you blink again!

Blinking spreads **tears** over your eyes. Tears protect your eyes and keep them from drying out. When you are calm, you may blink about 20 times a minute. If you are upset or excited, however, you might blink 100 times a minute. Luckily, the average blink lasts less than a second. So you don't even notice all those little moments of darkness.

The tears that spread during a blink come from special glands under your upper eyelids. Usually, just enough tears are made to keep your eyes moist. But sometimes you can get a real flood.

When you are very upset, you cry. Then tears flood your eyes and can overflow onto your face. Sometimes dust or other material gets into your eyes. Then your eyes fill with tears to wash the harmful substance away. Blinking fast often helps the tears do their job.

When you blink, your eyes close for a split second. But when you're scared you might squeeze them shut for a long time. Think about a ride on a roller coaster. You can close your eyes so you don't see what's coming next. But there's no fooling your stomach. It feels like it just flipped. In fact, you might be starting to feel dizzy . . .

when you suddenly wonder . . .

9

What causes motion sickness?

The roller coaster is making lots of turns. Your stomach starts to roll. Uh-oh, you think you're going to . . .

Just what is it about a moving vehicle that sometimes makes you feel so sick? You may be surprised to learn that the problem doesn't start in your stomach. It's in your head!

The trouble begins when your brain gets different messages. Let's say you are flying in an airplane and the ride gets bumpy. Structures inside your inner ear sense movement. Messages go to your brain saying that you are in motion.

However, sometimes what you feel is not the same as what you see. Inside the plane, your eyes see that the seats and walls are not moving. Your eyes send messages to your brain that you are still. Your brain can't make sense of the different information. That's when you may begin to feel sick.

Usually you can get used to the motion. Over time, your brain begins to make sense of things again. Your stomach settles down. In fact, you may be feeling cool and collected . . .

when you suddenly wonder . . .

Why do people sweat?

You're skateboarding down the path. It's a hot summer day. It looks like you've been swimming. But you haven't. You're just soaking wet with sweat!

You have about two million **sweat glands** all over your body. These sweat glands have tiny tubes that bring sweat from within your skin to the surface of your body. Why? It helps rid your body of heat.

When you exercise really hard, your body temperature rises. It's important to get rid of that extra heat. So your body has a built-in cooling system. How does it work? Well, as the water in sweat evaporates or drips off of you, it carries heat away from your body. This helps you to stay cool.

It's important to drink enough water every day to keep your cooling system working well. Which is easy to do when you're thirsty. In fact, you may be gulping down a large, cool drink . . .

when you suddenly wonder . . .

13

What causes hiccups?

You are sitting quietly in class. Suddenly a loud "hic" bursts from your mouth. You hold your breath but the hiccups keep coming.

They are a common problem, but scientists really don't know why we get the hiccups. Sometimes they start when we eat too much or drink too fast. Other times they seem to appear for no good reason.

So what causes these annoying little sounds? It all starts with the **diaphragm.** The diaphragm is a large muscle under the lungs in your chest. It lets you breathe in and out. When the diaphragm moves down, your lungs fill with air. When your diaphragm moves up, your lungs push air out.

Usually the diaphragm works smoothly in an up-and-down motion. But sometimes this big muscle can suddenly twitch. This causes you to take in a large gulp of air. When the air hits the vocal chords in your throat, the hiccup sound is made.

Most hiccups go away in a short period of time. But in some rare cases, they can go on for days or even weeks. The *Guinness Book of Records* says the longest case of hiccups lasted 69 years!

You have probably heard of many cures for the hiccups. In fact, you may be tired of holding your breath . . .

when you suddenly wonder . . .

Why do people need to sleep?

It's getting late. You're trying to finish a book. But your eyes start to feel very heavy. Only two more pages to go until . . . zzzzzzzzzzzz.

Sleeping is part of our natural daily rhythm. Our eyes close, our bodies relax. We do not respond to light or noise. Everything about us seems to slow down.

Everything, that is, except our brains. How do scientists know this? They attach a special machine to sleeping patients. This machine records brain waves.

Scientists found that there are several stages of sleep. During one stage of sleep, called **REM sleep,** our brains can be as active as they are when we are awake. We usually have three to five periods of REM sleep per night. This is when we have most of our dreams.

Surprisingly, scientists don't know exactly why we sleep. However, they have some good ideas. Many think that sleeping gives our body a "time out" so it can repair and build itself. Some chemicals that make you grow are released when you sleep. Other chemicals that help you fight disease are also more active when you rest.

Sleeping may also be important for learning. Some studies show that people remember things better after they "sleep on it."

You usually wake up in the morning feeling rested and refreshed. That is, unless you've had a scary dream. In fact, your heart may still be pounding from a nightmare . . .

Scientists use special wires and machines to study brain activity during sleep.

when you suddenly wonder . . .

17

What keeps your heart beating?

It starts to beat before you are born. It keeps on beating your entire life. What keeps this amazing organ going at such a steady pace?

Your heart is a muscle. But it's a different kind of muscle than the one in your arm or your leg. A healthy heart muscle doesn't get tired and it doesn't need to rest. It's a good thing, too. Your heart has an important job. It pumps blood through your entire body.

A group of special cells inside the heart keep it beating at a regular rate. These cells make up the **SA node.** The SA node delivers electrical signals to your heart.

This sets the pace of your heartbeat. For example, when you exercise, the SA node sends out more signals. This speeds up your heart rate. Then blood moving through your body can deliver oxygen more quickly to the muscles that are working so hard.

When we are scared, special chemicals are released in our body. These chemicals make the SA node fire out more signals. That's why your heart pounds after a nightmare. In fact, your mouth may get very dry with fear. You're getting a glass of water . . .

when you
suddenly
wonder . . .

What is saliva and how is it made?

Just thinking about your favorite sandwich can make your mouth fill with saliva. Saliva— commonly called "spit"—is mostly water. And it's more important than you might think.

Saliva is produced by structures called **salivary glands.** There are three pairs of large salivary glands that release saliva into our mouth. But that's not all. Smaller salivary glands also line our lips, cheeks, and tongue.

So why is saliva so important? First, it helps us digest food. When we taste, smell, or even think about food, our brain gives the order to release saliva. As soon as food enters our mouth, a special chemical in saliva goes to work. This chemical starts to break down starch in food. You may also have noticed that saliva gets food wet and slimy. This makes it much easier to swallow.

A healthy person's saliva also contains substances that may actually help fight disease. Scientists are busy studying saliva and learning more about what it does for our bodies. In fact, you may be thinking about what scientists are discovering . . .

when you
suddenly
wonder . . .

21

How can I find out more?

Read On!

Some of the most interesting books written about the human body are the ones that explain what goes on inside of you. If you want to learn more about your own "inner workings" you can look for these books at your library.

Cole, Joanna. *Magic School Bus: Inside the Human Body*. Scholastic, 1999.

Delafosse, Claude. *Human Body*. Scholastic, 2000.

Log On!

What makes dirty socks smell bad? Why do blue jeans look blue? To find out how your body smells, sees, hears, breathes, and much more, check out *www.kidshealth.org/kid/body/mybody.html* Just click on the topic you want to explore and you'll find yourself in the middle of pages and pictures all about your body. So keep your eyes open and the volume up because this website has sounds and animations that really bring your body to life!

Imagine That!

Were you surprised by any of the things you learned about your body in this book? Think about what interested you the most. Imagine that you are a newspaper reporter who needs to spread the word about this topic. Start with a "grabber" headline then write a short paragraph explaining what you want your readers to know.

Glossary

diaphragm—a large muscle beneath the lungs

follicle—a small tube in the skin from which hair grows

REM sleep—(Rapid Eye Movement sleep) a period of sleep during which the brain is very active and most dreams occur

SA node—a group of cells in the heart that send out electrical signals which make the heart pump

salivary glands—glands found in the mouth that produce saliva

sweat glands—glands found in the skin that produce sweat

tears—drops of liquid made by glands in the eyelids which keep the eyes moist